THE BEETLE
ALPHABET BOOK

Jerry Pallotta

Illustrated by David Biedrzycki

iai Charlesbridge

Thanks to John, Paul, George, Ringo, Mike, Al, Bruce, Dennis, Carl, and especially Brian.
—J. P.

To Kathy: All My Loving, Eight Days a Week, From Me to You, Honey Pie.
—D. B.

Published by Charlesbridge
85 Main Street
Watertown, MA 02472
(617) 926-0329
www.charlesbridge.com

Library of Congress Cataloging-in-Publication Data
Pallotta, Jerry.
  The beetle alphabet book / Jerry Pallotta ; illustrated by
David Biedrzycki.
     p. cm.
   Summary: Uses letters of the alphabet to introduce various
kinds of beetles.
      ISBN-13: 978-1-57091-551-2; ISBN-10: 1-57091-551-2 (reinforced for library use)
      ISBN-13: 978-1-57091-552-9; ISBN-10: 1-57091-552-0 (softcover)
1. Beetles—Juvenile literature. 2. English language—Alphabet—
Juvenile literature. [1. Beetles. 2. Alphabet.] I. Biedrzycki,
David, ill. II. Title.
QL576.2.P34 2004
595.76—dc21   2003008153

Printed in Korea
(hc) 10 9 8 7 6 5 4 3
(sc) 10 9 8 7 6

Celebrate! There is nothing on earth as diverse
as beetles. We start this alphabet book with the
heaviest beetle around.

Aa

A is for African Goliath Beetle.
This beetle is almost as large as your
hand. In Africa, children often tie strings
to these beetles and play with them as pets.

B b

B is for Bombardier Beetle. The Bombardier Beetle sprays poison gas to protect itself, but not enough to harm a person. Tiny bugs, teeny frogs, and little lizards should watch out!

C is for Cucumber Beetle. Farmers do not like this cute beetle because it eats tender young cucumber plants. Its cousins the Potato Beetle, the Asparagus Beetle, and the Carrot Beetle are also pests to farmers.

Cc

D is for Dung Beetle. Dung is poop. This beetle rolls balls of animal poop into its nest. It lays eggs in the poop so the babies will have something to eat when they hatch. Dung Beetles think poop is delicious.

D d

E is for Elephant Stag Beetle.
Beetles come in all different
shapes. These beetles look like
they have antlers. Come on
now! Behave! Stop fighting,
or you will be sent to the
principal's office.

Ee

Ff

F is for Fungus Beetle. This beetle needs to go to the beauty shop. It is not slick and shiny like many beetles. It is very difficult to recognize because it is camouflaged. It looks like decaying leaves, the bumpy bark of trees, or fungus.

G is for Giraffe Beetle. Wow! What a long neck!
The male Giraffe Beetle uses his unique neck to
roll up leaves. The female then lays her eggs in
this protected place.

Gg

Hh

H is for Harlequin Beetle. Its front legs are so huge, some people think they are its antennae. Beetles are insects. All insects have six legs.

Ii

I is for Ips Beetle. Most beetles are tiny. See if you can find the three Ips Beetles on the pine needles. Ips Beetles bore holes into trees. They look harmless, but they have been known to wipe out sections of forest.

Even though the word "bee" is inside
the word "beetle," a bee is not a beetle.
A beetle's wings fold inside its back. A
bee's wings are always on the outside.
Now buzz off, bee!

J is for June Bug. You can recognize a beetle by the straight line down its back. June Bugs usually appear in early summer during the month of June. That's how they got their name. How did you get your name?

J j

K k

K is for Kalahari Beetle. This Beetle lives in the Kalahari Desert where there is hardly any water. Name a place, and beetles probably live there. Mountains, plains, cities, beaches. Hot desert? Freezing nights? No problem.

L l

L is for Leaf Beetle. This beetle is the same color as the green leaves it eats for dinner. Leaf Beetles like to eat weeds and bushes more than trees. Some Leaf Beetles prefer the leaves of raspberries, strawberries, and grapes.

M is for Mexican Bean Beetle. This beetle is one of the largest ladybugs. It is a myth that the number of spots show how old a ladybug is. Most beetles live less than one year. It is not polite to ask a ladybug her age.

Mm

Are you looking at me?

I said, are you looking at me?

I am a spider, not a beetle. I am not even an insect.

Spiders have eight legs, not six. Spiders do not have wings.

N n

N is for Net-Winged
Beetle. Beetles have two
sets of wings. The hard
outer wings are called
elytra. In most beetles
the elytra are smooth and
shiny. The Net-Winged
Beetle has ridged elytra
that look like netting.

O is for Oriental Beetle. Scientists have discovered almost a million different species of beetles. There are more beetles on earth than any other type of creature. There are so many that you could probably write a thousand different beetle alphabet books.

P p

P is for Pie Dish Beetle. Other beetles have interesting names, too. There's the Furniture Beetle, the Drug Store Beetle, the Mud-Loving Beetle, the Death-Watch Beetle, and the Puffball Beetle. And here's more: the Flour Beetle, the Flower Beetle, the Snail-Eating Beetle, the Engraver Beetle, and the Ship Timber Beetle. Wow! Great names, great beetles!

Q is for Quartz Plain Beetle. This beetle blends in with its environment. It lives in the quartz plains where the rocks are white.

Rr

R is for Rhubarb Weevil. A weevil is a type of beetle that has a long snout. The most famous weevil of all is the Boll Weevil, which destroys cotton crops. Weevils are good at drilling holes into seeds, nuts, and fruit. Their teeth are at the end of their snouts.

S is for Seed Beetle. This Seed Beetle has comb-shaped antennae. Look through this book for examples of antennae diversity. You will find the thread type, the feather type, the ball-at-the-end type, the saw type, and the bead type.

Ss

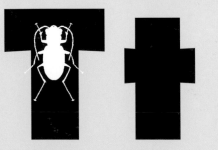

T is for Tiger Beetle. This
beetle has huge jaws. Beetles are
biters. Other insects have different
types of mouths. Butterflies are sippers,
house flies are spongers, grasshoppers are chewers,
bees are lickers, and mosquitoes are bloodsuckers.

U u

U is for Underwater Beetle. This beetle is like the U.S. Navy Seals. Sea! Air! Land! The Underwater Beetle can swim underwater, fly in the sky, and walk on land. Not many creatures can do that. Let's face it, beetles are amazing.

La Cucaracha! La Cucaracha!
Don't be fooled. Cockroaches are not beetles.
Can you see the difference? The wings of a
cockroach overlap.

Vv

V is for Violin Beetle.
Here is another crazy-shaped
beetle. It looks like a violin. Let's
see . . . if we had a Viola Beetle,
a Cello Beetle, and two Violin Beetles,
we would have a beetle string quartet. A
Violin Beetle can also be called a Guitar Beetle.

W is for Whirligigs.
Whirligigs dance on top of
ponds and streams. They look
like bumper cars going every which way.
Whirligigs can see above and below the water at
the same time. Remember—beetles can fly. If they
get tired of one pond, they just fly over to another.

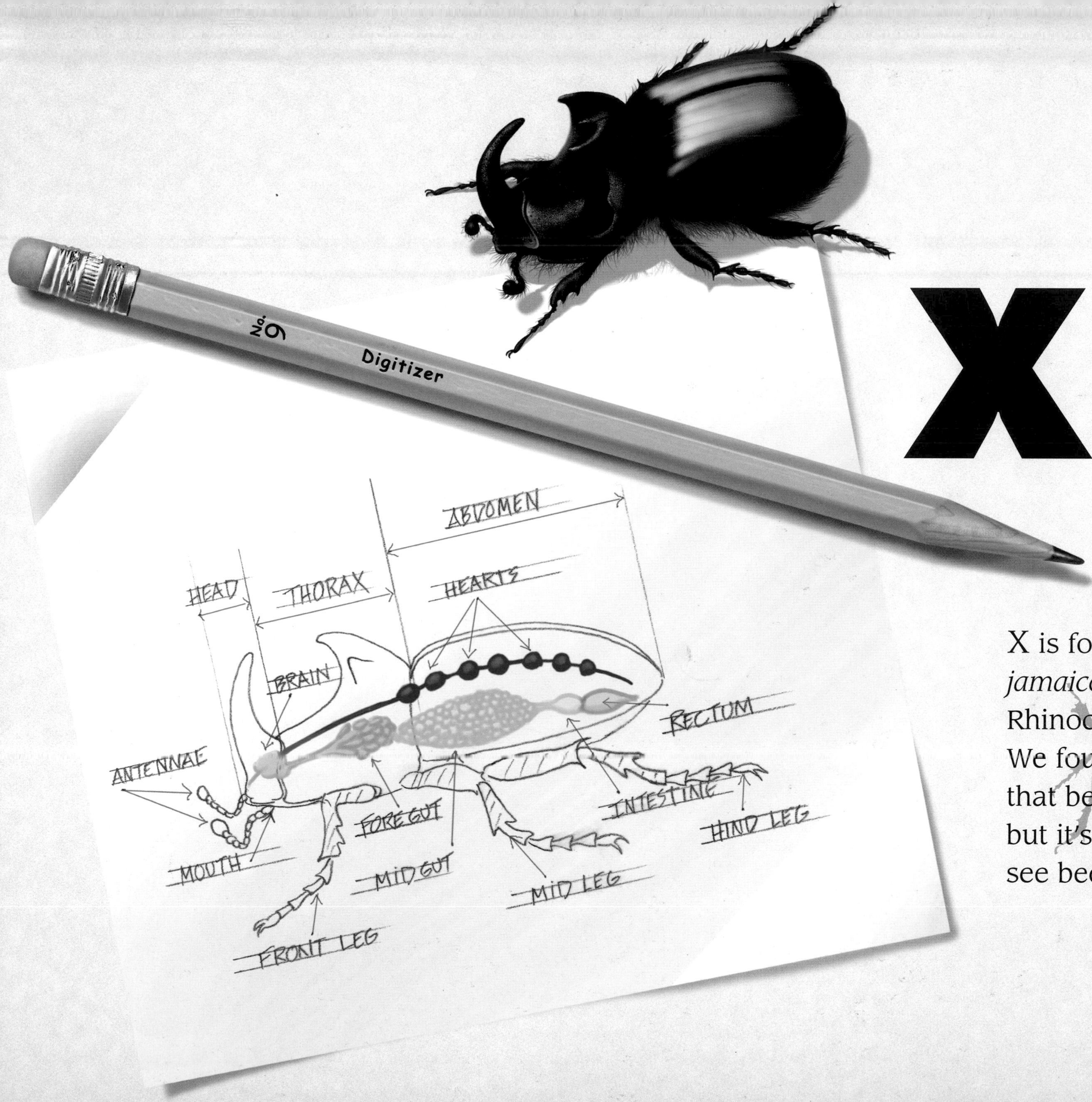

Xx

X is for *Xyloryctes jamaicensis*, a Rhinoceros Beetle. We found a beetle that begins with "X," but it's more fun to see beetle guts.

Diagram labels:

ABDOMEN

HEAD

THORAX

HEARTS

BRAIN

ANTENNAE

RECTUM

MOUTH

FOREGUT

INTESTINE

MIDGUT

HIND LEG

MID LEG

FRONT LEG

No. 9 Digitizer

Yy

Y is for Yellow Tortoise Beetle. Are you ready for some big words? People who study insects and bugs are called entomologists. If they specialize in beetles, they are called coleopterists. Maybe you'll be a coleopterist when you grow up.

Welcome to the land of Metallic Beetles. Did someone forget some jewelry? On this page there is a Zinc Metallic Beetle, a Platinum Metallic Beetle, a Gold Metallic Beetle, a Silver Metallic Beetle, and a Bronze Metallic Beetle. Z is for Zinc Metallic Beetle.

The Engraver Beetles were here!
They left us a message.